AN ILLUSTRATED GUIDE TO
COCKTAILS

AN ILLUSTRATED GUIDE TO
COCKTAILS

50 Classic Cocktail Recipes, Tips, and Tales

ORR SHTUHL

Illustrated by Elizabeth Graeber

GOTHAM
BOOKS

GOTHAM BOOKS
Published by the Penguin Group
Penguin Group (USA) Inc., 375 Hudson Street,
New York, New York 10014, USA

USA | Canada | UK | Ireland | Australia | New Zealand | India | South Africa | China
Penguin Books Ltd, Registered Offices: 80 Strand, London WC2R 0RL, England
For more information about the Penguin Group visit penguin.com.

LIBRARY OF CONGRESS CATALOGING-IN-PUBLICATION DATA
has been applied for.

ISBN 978-1-592-40795-8

Printed in the United States of America
10 9 8 7 6 5 4 3 2 1

Set in Haarlemmer MT Std with Gotham

Designed by DANIEL LAGIN

While the author has made every effort to provide accurate telephone numbers, Internet addresses, and other contact information at the time of publication, neither the publisher nor the author assumes any responsibility for errors or for changes that occur after publication. Further, the publisher does not have any control over and does not assume any responsibility for author or third-party websites or their content.

To all cocktail drinkers,
from the sage imbiber to the budding enthusiast.

INTRODUCTION

A classic cocktail is made of three parts: something strong (liquor), something sweet (like sugar or a liqueur), and something bitter (oddly, we just call those "bitters"). You can find these elements even in a simple gin and tonic, where rough juniper mellows into the dual sugar-sweet and quinine bitterness of tonic, finished with a tart spike of lime.

Strong, sweet, and bitter—a good cocktail has the intrigue of a drama, the joy of a salty-sweet dessert, and the sin of alluring vice. From the bawdy innkeepers of the eighteenth century to the gangster bootleggers of Prohibition, liquor has always had its characters, and cocktails are the keepers of the lore. Some creation legends include tales of the poker hustler Jack Rose, the famous matador film *Blood and Sand*, and a club dancer named Margarita Carmen Cansino, who eventually became the pinup actress known as Rita Hayworth.

Where there's a drink, there's a story. We love reading them, and we enjoy them all the more with a nice cocktail in hand. These are some of our favorites, and we hope you like them too.

OLD-FASHIONED

Theories abound for the origins of the word "cocktail," some deriving from the French word for an eggcup (*coquetier*), some involving creative uses for a rooster's tail feather, and some employing a color of humor not suitable for polite publication. Originally (sometime around 1800), "cocktail" actually meant an Old-Fashioned as we know it today. But the end of the nineteenth century saw an explosion of new "cocktails," using juices and vermouths and any number of spirits. Amid this proliferation, the exasperated drinker took to ordering an "old-

1½ ounces bourbon or rye
1 teaspoon simple syrup
2 dashes Angostura bitters

➜ Stir in a short glass over ice and garnish with a lemon twist.

fashioned cocktail" when they wanted a no-frills glass of whiskey, sugar, bitters, and ice. It's not so much a recipe as it is a method of doctoring up a spirit, as one completes a dish with dashes of salt and pepper. It's the original cocktail.

Winston Churchill's mother

MANHATTAN

If the Old-Fashioned first took the edge off a spirit with sugar, the borough-named drinks of New York advanced this concept twice over, introducing vermouth and orange juice to the mix. At the center of this family (and indeed, the center of cocktail genealogy altogether) is the Manhattan.

Like the Old-Fashioned, the history of the Manhattan is fractured, and my favorite version is one historians have deemed unlikely. But why let accuracy stand between us and a good story? This version pegs the drink's inception to the aptly named Manhattan Club in New York, where sometime in the 1870s Winston Churchill's mother, Jeanette, threw a gala honoring the newly elected governor, Samuel J. Tilden. It turns out that even if Tilden was received with Manhattan cocktails, Lady Churchill probably wasn't there herself. But the club was a serious purveyor of mixed drinks, and it still contends for the honor of invention with another, an unnamed bar near the corner of Bowery and Houston. So while we don't know for certain which mahogany den first sprung the union of spirit and vermouth, we know it was at least on the island of the same name.

We also know it took off with the tippling public, and it's easy to see why—the silky, sweetened mixture of whiskey, vermouth, and bitters is a good deal more sociable than the day's other style of drinking liquor: neat, and with force.

2 ounces bourbon or rye
1 ounce sweet vermouth
2–3 dashes Angostura bitters

→ Stir with ice and strain into a
cocktail glass. Toast to forgotten
inventors everywhere.

WHY LET ACCURACY STAND BETWEEN US AND A GOOD STORY?

The Manhattan, the Bronx & the Brooklyn
— The New York Boroughs —

Bronx

Manhattan

Brooklyn

lemon & lime

orange juice and gin

Vermouth

cocktail

Breakfast

WA
WALDORF
ASTORIA

Lunch

pink elephant ↓

BRONX

For the hard drinkers, spirits were taking a problematic turn toward the hoity-toity. First, barmen tainted them with sugar and bitters. Then they gussied them up with vermouth, that weak tipple of old maids. What would be next, dessert? Apparently so.

By the end of the nineteenth century, lemon and lime juice were accepted cocktail ingredients—their sharp acidity could cut through heavy syrups and stand up to spicy liquor. But the Bronx cocktail piled on not only sweet and dry vermouth but now *orange juice* to a beleaguered shot of gin. This was too much for traditionalists to take, but it hit big-time popularity, finding its way on to hotel and gala menus as a

civilized, less boozy means of taking one's gin. This also made it a more acceptable drink for earlier in the day, with lunch, or sometimes even before noon.

The recipe comes from Johnnie Solon, who manned the bar at the Waldorf Astoria during its heyday. Challenged by a customer to invent a new drink, he started with a Duplex, his bar's mix of sweet and dry vermouth, shaken with orange bitters and a strip of peel, and added to it a jigger of parts gin and juice. The name was inspired not by the borough but by the animals at the zoo therein, a cocktailian nod to the pink elephants and other "strange animals" his customers told of seeing after a few too many drinks. His clientele took to it as a lunchtime beverage, and according to Solon, it wasn't long before the restaurant churned through a case of oranges a day. Elsewhere, some saw the OJ as an invitation to morning drinking—including President William Howard Taft.

1½ ounces gin
¾ ounce orange juice
¼ ounce sweet vermouth
¼ ounce dry vermouth

→ Shake with ice and strain into a cocktail glass as part of a complete breakfast.

WILLIAM HOWARD TAFT

He's best known to today's schoolchildren as the three-hundred-pound president who managed to imprison himself in the White House bathtub, but President Taft attracted a reputation for gluttony throughout his administration. In 1911, he caused a stir by drinking Bronx cocktails at a breakfast meeting with clergymen in St. Louis. (Though they labeled the meal a "*déjeuner*," French for "lunch," perhaps to make the drinking more seemly.)

Chronicling the controversy, however, a *New York Times* writer sided with the president, needling the clergymen for not being familiar with the drink. Noting that a college graduate would surely have learned his way around cocktails while at university, he couldn't help but make assumptions as to their educational background. "Our universities are doing their duty in this respect," the author wrote. "Can it be possible that these Missouri clergymen are not college men?"

BROOKLYN

But back to whiskey. Unlike its brethren boroughs, Brooklyn required several attempts at an eponymous cocktail before one stuck. (Queens and Staten Island remain open to interpretation by the bartenders of tomorrow.) First, at the Schmidt Cafe near the Brooklyn side of the Brooklyn Bridge, a Cincinnati transplant named Maurice Hegeman served a pint glass of hard cider and ginger ale soiled by an incongruous shot of absinthe. Next, the Hotel Nassau in Long Beach tried to popularize a mix of gin with sweet and dry vermouths buoyed with a spoonful of raspberry syrup, but drinkers were not yet receptive to such candied flavors. Scoffed one barkeep at the Waldorf Astoria: "All he forgot was the ice cream."

Finally, a recipe emerged, published in a few books around 1910 in the form that we recognize today. If it's a delicious cocktail (it is), that's because it's a modified Manhattan—and one of many to be coined throughout the century.

hard
cider → ← ginger ale

← absinthe

"All he forgot was
the ice cream"

HOW TO LIKE WHISKEY (U.S. VERSION)

Ah, whiskey, that quintessential of American liquors (as long as it's spelled with an "E"). In bourbon, you have the bottled essence of amber waves of grain: rolling hills of chewy barley and sweet corn. In rye, a rough-hewn cousin: the pure distillation of our pioneering spirit.

But it's not always easy for a curious drinker to tame whiskey's wild spirit, and plenty of people have seen their appetite for it vanish after a poorly made Manhattan or a Jack-and-Coke-fueled hangover. Whether you're looking to get reacquainted or starting afresh, here's a curriculum of cocktails that make room for people of all tastes on the whiskey wagon.

BEGINNER: JACK ROSE (PAGE 44)

OK, so this is cheating a bit—we're using applejack, and not whiskey at all. But this American style of apple brandy is a good introduction to the rocky, woodsy sweetness of bourbon and other American whiskeys. Grenadine and lemon team up for a

WHISKEY   WHISKY
American   British

sweet-tart drink that's safe for even the most cautious beginner. Just get started, already!

ADVANCED: INVERSE MANHATTAN (PAGE 7)

The classic Manhattan is, well, a classic. But it's a big glass of mostly whiskey, and not always suitable for polite company. Flipping the ratio—two parts vermouth to one part liquor—gets you a drink that's friendly for curious drinkers and makes a nice aperitif even for die-hard whiskey lovers.

EXPERT: OLD-FASHIONED (PAGE 3)

There's simply no other correct answer. This is the original cocktail: Take a spirit, add sugar and a touch of bitters. There's a reason this recipe has held up for so long. If you haven't had one yet, do so immediately.

Martini, Martinez, and Dry Martini

Be honest: You picked up this book and turned straight to this page, didn't you? I don't blame you; the ubiquitous Martini is nearly synonymous with the word "cocktail." And to most people, the V-shaped stemware it arrives in is a "Martini glass," even though it's still a good home for an Aviation or a Manhattan. And speaking of Manhattans, if you did take the direct route to this page, you might want to bookmark that section for later, because believe it or not, that elemental whiskey-vermouth-bitters drink is where the king of cocktails got its start.

Today, for many, shall we say, "mission-driven" drinkers, a

Proud martini drinker

Martini is an excuse to consume as much gin as possible. Misguided folks will boast tragically about their preferred strength of Martini, leading to an arms race that ends in glasses of icy gin with a slight whiff of the dry vermouth they poured down a nearby drain. In hard times, this can be a fine drink, but one I would call "Cold Gin," not a Martini.

In fact, the Martini began not only as a more palatable cocktail but one that didn't shy away from sugar. After the Manhattan's success, bartenders began combining vermouth with other spirits, and gin in particular caught on. This was in the 1880s, when the vermouth in question was sweet vermouth, and the gin was Old Tom, a sweetened style from England that came out rounder than the now-standard London Dry. So the earliest Martinis were rosy affairs that looked something like this:

ORIGINAL MARTINI

1½ ounces Old Tom gin
1½ ounces sweet vermouth
dash of orange bitters (Regan's for subtlety, Angostura Orange if you're feeling feisty)

➜ Stir over ice and strain. Garnish freely with a twist of orange or lemon.

And in practice, many bartenders added a small dose of sugar syrup to *that*. Then, originating in the same decade, you have the Martinez, a more developed recipe that's centered around vermouth and accented with the marzipan notes of maraschino liqueur.

MARTINEZ

2 ounces sweet vermouth
1 ounce Old Tom gin
1 teaspoon maraschino*
dash of orange bitters

→ Stir over ice and strain.
   Again, a twist wouldn't hurt.

ut I know what you were really looking for: a Dry Martini. That is, the clear kind, served with olives or a twist and classier than a white tuxedo. These emerged around the turn of the (twentieth) century as gin gained popularity in America, especially the "London Dry" style of gin we think of as standard today. As our Martinis got drier, so did our other cocktails.

---

* Maraschino liqueur, most often found under the Luxardo brand, is made from unpitted marasca cherries, which impart a sort of almondy flavor. It has no relation to the fluorescent cherries preserved in melted candy—if you have those in your cupboard, spare your cocktails and use them on your next gingerbread house.

Cocktails like the Manhattan were often doctored with sugar syrup early on, but soon the once-ubiquitous syrup disappeared from nearly everything but the Old-Fashioned. A sweet tooth became the mark of a country bumpkin; the urbane drinker wanted everything dry. Cutting out sugar let the taste of a refined spirit shine through; on the other hand, if you drank with the vigor of that day's social elite, it also made the night's eleventh and twelfth drinks easier on your stomach.

As I mentioned, some people testify to mixing Dry Martinis with two ingredients, gin and ice. But the dry vermouth is not so much the sugar in your coffee as it is the jelly in a PB&J. The Dry Martini is an exercise in balance, and while everyone should mix to their own taste, I'd hope this means you actually can taste both ingredients. Personally, I often like my Dry Martinis 50-50, or equal parts gin and vermouth—but then, I like vermouth more than the average person. If you're too thirsty to decide, a basic 2-to-1 ratio is a good starting point.

DRY MARTINI

2 ounces gin
1 ounce dry vermouth

→ Stir with ice and strain into a cocktail glass, then
garnish with a twist (lemon by default, though I like
orange with some softer gins). I'd rather eat olives
than drop them in my wine, but there's no shame in
the salty route if that's the mood you're in.

The humble author of this book does not generally cast judgment on the tastes of an agent of espionage as accomplished as James Bond. However, it does come as a disappointment that one of the most famous of all Martini drinkers has an etiquette of imbibing that, for the last four decades, has flown in the case of tradition, even reason.

First, a Martini is made with gin, never vodka. Second, while Mr. Bond's field repertoire might shun the delicate touch espoused by the rest of the operatives at MI6, his tastes needn't lack the same refinement. A proper Martini is always stirred, gently chilling and diluting the spirits without the jarring shards of ice produced by vigorous shaking. Spare the bartender while ordering your own Martinis; not all men in tuxedos are cut for Mr. Bond's violent, brutish flourishes.

Fortunately, when Daniel Craig assumed the persona in 2006 with *Casino Royale*, he also brought with him a more refined palate, replacing the ersatz Martini with a very serious cocktail named the Vesper. Thanks, Mr. Bond.

VESPER

**3 ounces gin
1 ounce vodka
½ ounce Lillet Blanc**

➔ Stir (see?) and strain into cocktail glass.

MINT JULEP

The Mint Julep's history is a well-documented one, but to properly construct and enjoy this drink, you don't need to know that the word derives from the Persian and Arabic words for rose water, or that a South Carolinian named William Heyward Trapier is honored annually at the University of Oxford for having introduced the drink to its student body. Neither do you need a heavy silver cup, a celebrated horse race, nor an anachronistic seersucker suit. No, to bury your nose in a bouquet of leaves and sip nectared bourbon through a crush of ice, all you need is whiskey, sugar, and a bunch of fresh mint. However, through scientific methods I have determined that these ingredients are best when combined on a warm, sunny afternoon.

3 ounces bourbon
¾ ounce simple syrup
fresh mint

→ Muddle mint leaves in a glass and fill
with crushed ice. Add bourbon and
simple syrup, and garnish with another
copious bouquet of mint.

I introduce to you, the

MINT JULEP

A Small Amount of Information About Simple Syrup and Citrus Juice

SIMPLE SYRUP

Simple syrup is just sugar water. The recipes in this book (and in general, nearly all cocktail recipes) call for sugar and water in equal parts. There are two ways to make this:

- Boil water and stir in sugar until dissolved.
- Combine lukewarm water and sugar in a jar and shake until dissolved.

I prefer the shake method because it's ready to use immediately; if you boil, you should cool the syrup to room temperature

before using so you don't melt the ice in your cocktail. In your fridge, simple syrup will keep for a month, and then some.

CITRUS JUICE

Oranges, lemons, limes, and the like should be squeezed fresh for cocktails. If you want to squeeze a lot in advance, do it shortly before serving—fresh juice begins to oxidize and lose its flavor after a few hours.

When shopping, look for thin-skinned and supple lemons and limes, which tend to be juiciest. For oranges, Valencias are fantastic.

freshly squeezed juice

JERRY THOMAS

n 1862, Jerry Thomas published *How to Mix Drinks, or the Bon Vivant's Companion*, the seminal guide for which we today consider him the founding father of cocktail bartending. Turns out he held himself in high esteem, too.

In addition to studying at bars across the country, from San Francisco to Chicago to St. Louis to New Orleans, he also toured Europe—and brought with him his signature set of solid silver bar tools. By the time he authored his guide, the country's most prominent cocktailian commanded a higher salary than that of America's vice president, and had led such famed barrooms as New York's Metropolitan Hotel and St. Louis's Planter's House.

Just how highly did he think of himself? In his book's introduction, he proclaims that his name alone is "sufficient guarantee" of perfection—then he compares himself to England's great bard: "'Good wine needs no bush,' Shakespeare tells us and over one of Jerry's mixtures eulogy is quite as redundant."

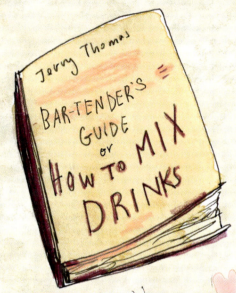

Jerry Thomas

BAR-TENDER'S
GUIDE
or
How to MIX
DRINKS

fill with:
juices, syrups,
liquors + ice cubes

shake↑

pour

BLUE BLAZER

The Blue Blazer is a dangerous drink to make. Additionally, it doesn't taste particularly good. But perhaps no other cocktail in Jerry Thomas's oeuvre better exemplifies the master bartender's flair for flair, and as such, the budding connoisseur may ignite and extinguish this sticky-sweet Scotch mixture, if only as an homage. Just be careful not to set your house on fire.

HOW TO MAKE A BLUE BLAZER
WITHOUT SETTING YOUR HOUSE ON FIRE

(serves 2)

4 ounces Scotch (the higher proof, the better)
3 ounces hot water
1 tablespoon sugar (or a splash of simple syrup)
two mugs (handles strongly recommended)
fire, or an implement with which to create it

➔ Gather some friends you'd like to impress. (You'll want a character witness if your neighbor catches you tossing about a stream of flaming whiskey.)

➔ Pour the Scotch, water, and sugar into a mug. Traditionally, these are pewter or silver, but anything heat-safe will do. Tulip-shaped mugs make for easier pouring, and of course handles are helpful.

➔ Turn the lights off and prepare your friends to be awed.

➔ Ignite the drink by holding a lit match or lighter to the alcohol fumes over the mug.

➔ Pour the flaming mix back and forth between the mugs, never quite emptying either mug so that each carries an eternal flame of alcohol. Bask in the impressed sighs of your guests.

➔ Pour all the liquid into one mug, and extinguish the flame by tamping the empty mug onto the full one. Pour into two small glasses.

➔ Confirm that all the flames are out, your curtains aren't burning, and your cat is safe and sound.

➔ Garnish with lemon twists and serve.

Note: Playing with fire is serious business. Make sure to take necessary precautions, like having someone to take glamour photos of you, and not telling your parents and/or worrywart spouse until after you've finished.

JACK ROSE

This sweet, puckery cocktail, one of the smoothest of classic lore, is also one with blood on its hands. Its apocryphal namesake is Bald Jack Rose, gangster, poker player, and bagman for the crooked Lt. Charles Becker of the New York Police Department's antigambling squad in the 1910s. Rose became a minor celebrity in the high-profile murder trial of Herman Rosenthal, a gambler whose debt to Becker led to his murder—a hit Rose himself orchestrated. After a shifty deal with the prosecutors, Rose went free, his testimony sending Lt. Becker and four unsympathetic murderers to the electric chair.

At least, that's one story. The crime and trial really happened, but the cocktail's name more likely comes from the lovely Jacquemot rose flower, and its provenance could not be more esteemed: The Jack Rose was originally served at the high-society parties at Manhattan's gilded Astor mansion.

1½ ounces applejack
½ ounce lemon juice
¼ ounce grenadine

➔ Shake menacingly and strain
into a cocktail glass.

No, no. It's
A P P L E J A C K

GEORGE WASHINGTON

Times were simpler in the early days of the United States. They didn't have cocktails; when they drank liquor, they drank it neat or with a little water. Both politicians and populace would imbibe freely and publicly; the average adult drank three times more than today. This helped the nation's first president ease into retirement from the White House, founding a rye distillery at his estate at Mount Vernon that became the nation's largest, producing 11,000 gallons annually—a feat that made him, we can only assume, the world's first war-hero-turned-father-of-democracy-turned-commercial distiller.

CHERRY BOUNCE

And here's a historian's tip: Add "George Washington ate this" to anything for instant credibility. Fortunately, he enjoyed drinking, too. Beer, rye whiskey, and heaps of punch recipes were all in rotation at the Washingtons' household, but there's another less common tipple that Martha Washington had her own recipe for: Cherry Bounce.

Cherry Bounce is a basic infusion—the cherries and booze mingle for a very long time until their flavors get friendly. But which sound more enticing, a scientific "infusion" or a sweet glass of "bounce"?

750 milliliters bourbon or brandy
1 quart cherries
1 cup sugar

→ Combine the above in a big jar with a lid, and let the flavors mingle for at least a month (though more is better). When your patience has run out, serve neat.

The cherries make all the difference here, so I like to use sour pie cherries right at the best part of summer (cherry season) and open it during the holidays. You'll probably want to add more sugar, but it's harder to remove sugar than it is to add it, so start with just a cup. Some people gussy it up by adding allspice or nutmeg to the infusion, but that's letting your precious cherries die in vain. Love them for who they are.

BOUNCE

BETTY FLANAGAN

For much of history, women bartenders have been embattled by their colleagues, customers, and even the Supreme Court—many states banned them from the profession well after suffrage was achieved, into the 1950s and 1960s. But American women behind the bar have a tradition dating back to the nation's birth.

Betty Flanagan was a New York innkeeper in the late eighteenth century, left alone after her husband died in the Revolutionary War. A revolutionary herself, she was no friend of the British—including her neighbor, a poor, English chicken farmer. So when a troupe of American and French soldiers marched in one evening, looking for rooms and carrying suspiciously fresh roosters, Flanagan was happy to oblige in preparing a feast for the boarders' dinner. The luxuriant meal was capped with a round of drinks, each one stirred with a rooster's tail feather. As the soldiers celebrated their vanquishing of the local English foothold, they raised their glasses and cheered, bellowing to their host for "another cock-tail!"

FISH HOUSE PUNCH

The idea of filling a considerable bowl with alcohol, sugar, citrus, and spice predates the cocktail by several centuries, and the subject alone could fill several books. (Indeed, it already has.) So if there's only room for one punch recipe here, it may as well be one of the nation's first and grandest.

The Fish House is the estate of the United States' oldest social club: the State in Schuylkill, founded in Philadelphia in 1732. As the name might indicate, it was (and still is) a fishing club, and its members would from time to time dip their poles into the waters of the Schuylkill River with some intention of a catch. But the members of this society were best known for their lavish parties, and records indicate that they were more the gastronome type than they were hunters and gatherers.

The club entertained scores of elites, including senators and

FISH HOUSE PUNCH, SOCIABLE VERSION

(about 50 servings)

one 750-milliliter bottle light rum
one 750-milliliter bottle dark rum
one 750-milliliter bottle applejack
2–3 cups simple syrup
2–3 cups lemon juice (about 14 lemons)
3–4 cups iced tea
3–4 cups apple cider

ambassadors, foreign dignitaries, leaders of business, and (at least as of 1905) ten American presidents. Their first was George Washington, and seemingly, he was also their favorite, as every occasion at the Fish House begins with a toast to the Founding Father. As Fish House Punch is the club's official drink, it appears at every event as well, and likely by the bowlful. After Washington attended his honorary dinner at the State in Schuylkill, his diary marks off three blank pages, perhaps a testament to the days of recovery that follow such a feast.

A favorite annual dinner ritual was when the oldest son of each member would be "baptized" in the club's most precious china bowl, filled with the official punch. Whether this meant a mere sip or a literal soaking is hard to determine from historical records. But whatever your intentions are, always make this recipe in quantity, just in case the occasion calls for an emergency blessing.

Compare the recipe below with historical versions, and you'll see several differences, the first of which is that the real thing had no tea and no cider—it was only booze, sugar, and lemon. Another difference is that the early Americans used a spirit they called peach brandy, which was a far cry from today's sugary schnapps, and is no longer available. So here is an updated recipe that swaps the peaches for apples and dilutes the mixture for the sake of your guests. It's not going to earn any certificates of authenticity, but it's very good.

HOW TO BUY BAR EQUIPMENT

For the devoted shopper, the number of fanciful stirrers, strainers, shakers, jiggers, and other implements available for purchase on the way to building your home bar is limitless. (Not to even mention glassware.)

On the other end of the spectrum, you can make an Old-Fashioned with just a jigger and a spoon. Add a shaker and a strainer, and you can mix up most of the classics.

Here are the three levels of stocking equipment for your home bar. Where you start is up to you, but a word of warning: Buying cocktail equipment is addictive. You might start with a pair of shakers, but before long you're spending weekends alone with the classified section, scouring for eighteen-piece punch sets in Depression glass. And I'll understand.

LEVEL 1: JUST GET ME AN OLD-FASHIONED.

You can turn out Old-Fashioneds, Manhattans, Martinis, and most other classics with just four pieces of equipment. Anything else is frippery.

- **jigger:** Measurements are key. A standard shot size is 1.5 ounces, but get a graduated jigger, and you'll only need one.

- **Boston shaker:** aka big metal cup to mix and shake in. (To shake, jam a beer glass into the top.) Metal is important because it turns cold quicker.

- **Hawthorne strainer:** aka the springy kind. The name comes from the original inventor's Boston cafe . . . ah, just Google it.

- **barspoon:** I prefer stirring with a chopstick, but barspoons also double as a teaspoon measure.

Boston shaker

Jigger

Graduated jigger ↑

Hawthorne shaker

Barspoon ↑

LEVEL 2: LET'S HAVE SOME FUN.

Stroll through the "implements" aisle of your cocktail supply store (you live near one, right?), and you'll quickly find more toys than you ever thought you'd need. Well, you need them.

☐ **citrus juicer:** squeeze

☐ **zester:** garnish (veggie peeler works too)

☐ **muddler:** someone's going to want a Mojito

☐ **tea strainer:** keep out the ice shards

☐ **squeeze bottle:** keep your simple syrup

☐ **tumblers:** for anything on ice

☐ **coupes:** for anything not on ice

Citrus juicer: squeeze

Muddler:
someone's gonna
want a
Mojito.

barspoon: stir

JIGGER SET

Zester: garnish

Hawthorne Shaker.
strain

Boston Shaker:
pour

tumblers: for anything on ice

Squeeze bottle: keep your
simple syrup.

Tea Strainer:
Keep out the ice shards

Coupes: for anything not on ice

Pewter mug:

SHOPPING!

HOORAY!

LEVEL 3: SHOPPING!

- ☐ **swizzle stick**
- ☐ **long glasses**
- ☐ **punch set**
- ☐ **pewter mugs**
- ☐ **julep strainer**
- ☐ **ice crushing bag**
- ☐ **three-part shaker**
- ☐ **speed pourers**
- ☐ **ice pick**
- ☐ **cocktail picks**

long glass

Absinthe fountain & spoon

empty basket ←

COCKTAIL MAKING SUPPLIES:

- jigger set
- Boston shaker ??
- Hawthorne strainer
- barspoon
- citrus juicer
- zester muddler
- tea strainer
- squeeze bottle
- tumblers
- coupes
- long glasses
- pewter mugs
- punch set
- mason jars

- swizzel stick
- ice pick
- cocktail picks
- Absinth fountain
- three parts shaker
- speed pourer
- seltzer maker
- dropper bottle.

★ ALCOHOL ★

Glasses

Absinthe fountain & spoon

dropper bottle

wine fridge

Julep strainer

pewter mug

cocktail picks

long glasses :

seltzer maker

- [ ] seltzer maker
- [ ] absinthe fountain and spoon
- [ ] dropper bottle
- [ ] mason jars
- [ ] wine fridge

BONUS! LEVEL 0: I LIVE IN SQUALOR.

Maybe you just moved, and all your stuff is in boxes. Or maybe your kitchen is literally empty except for some "repurposed" takeout containers and a commemorative plastic cup from your 1988 trip to Sea World. Here's how to make a Martini using exactly those things.

Fill Sea World commemorative cup with ice.

In Sea World commemorative cup, add 2 ounces gin and 1 ounce dry vermouth. (In absence of measuring utensil, count 2 ounces by pouring at a medium pace while slowly saying "Sea World commemorative cup" one time. For 1 ounce, just say "commemorative.")

Stir, using one chopstick from preserved takeout bag. (If no chopstick is available, use plastic utensil or Sea World commemorative straw.)

Fit plastic lid onto Sea World commemorative cup, pour drink through straw hole into your favorite glass, coffee mug, or cereal bowl, and enjoy.

SEA WORLD COMMEMORATIVE CUP

Sea World Commemorative cup

one chop stick OR one plastic utensil

COMMEMORATIVE

CORPSE REVIVER #2

Corpse Reviver #1 was a droll blend of brandy, sweet vermouth, and applejack, so it's no wonder that it collected dust while its successor made a comeback. Drinking your first Corpse Reviver #2 is like glimpsing a mythical creature. It's a fantastical, transcendental experience that inspires sonnets and arias, a liquid potion of poetry wherein Lillet sprites dance with absinthe fairies in an endless meadow of orange blossoms, waltzing through a world that knows only summer solstice and endless skies.

But I don't want to oversell it, see for yourself:

¾ ounce gin
¾ ounce Cointreau
¾ ounce Lillet Blanc
¾ ounce lemon juice
1 dash absinthe

➜ Shake with ice and strain, then bring the salve to your lips as you brace for sensory perfection. When this dramatically titled cocktail was invented at London's famous Savoy Hotel by Harry Craddock, he created it as a hangover cure. The bliss it summons will erase from your mind not only a hangover but also the very idea of a world with evil.

BILL McCOY

S tock car racing is famously borne of the Prohibition, when Appalachian bootleggers lightened their cars to outpace their pursuers. But the premium spirits were smuggled en masse by ship from the Caribbean, where liquor could still be obtained lawfully. (These authentic bottles of whiskey, gin, and rum had the additional advantage of being free of poison fillers, like formaldehyde.) McCoy himself didn't even drink, but being a yacht-builder and freighter, he saw an opportunity in oceanic bootlegging when his other business dried up. He grew a reputation for selling only pure products, and soon his name became an appellation for authenticity of any kind, known henceforth as "the real McCoy."

THE
· REAL M^cCOY ·

BLOODY MARY

In case you were wondering, there is such a thing as a healthy cocktail. Invented by a Parisian named Fernand Petiot in 1921, the Bloody Mary is a veritable food pyramid of a drink. Tomatoes? Some say vegetable and some say fruit, so let's count it as both. Salt? If your body doesn't get 180 milligrams a day, you could die. Worcestershire sauce? That's in the pyramid somewhere, maybe in one of the corners. Alcohol is a critical social lubricant, and hot pepper is good for the humors. Garnish with celery, and this drink is practically guaranteed to raise your life expectancy.

Speaking of garnishes, this is the cocktail for unleashing your wildest fancy snacks. Grab a toothpick and go pantry hunting for savory to crown your fiery long drinks. If you need inspiration, try this garnish wheel:

[GARNISH WHEEL]

- celery
- carrots
- pickled okra
- pickled onion
- olives
- beef jerky
- olives with garlic
- shrimp
- Old Bay seasoning
- cheese cubes
- potato chips
- olives with the red cubes that are peppers but feel like jelly
- General Tso's chicken
- lemon wedge
- lime wedge
- pig in a blanket

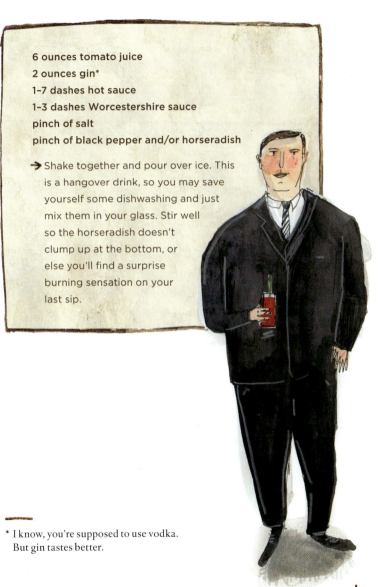

6 ounces tomato juice

2 ounces gin*

1–7 dashes hot sauce

1–3 dashes Worcestershire sauce

pinch of salt

pinch of black pepper and/or horseradish

→ Shake together and pour over ice. This is a hangover drink, so you may save yourself some dishwashing and just mix them in your glass. Stir well so the horseradish doesn't clump up at the bottom, or else you'll find a surprise burning sensation on your last sip.

* I know, you're supposed to use vodka. But gin tastes better.

SCREWDRIVER

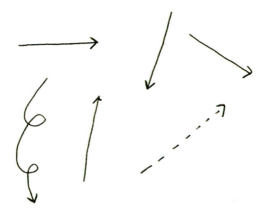

It's a telling indication that, at press time, the Wikipedia page for "Screwdriver (cocktail)" shows a photo of a wan, yellow mixture inhabiting an undistinguished tumbler on a faux-wood tabletop in an Alabama airport. In such sad scenarios, the thirsty traveler may have no choice but to resort to this lonely mix of vodka and orange juice. But when times are better, and you're looking for a cocktail to celebrate the sweet pucker of an orange, allow me to direct you to . . .

MIMOSA

ggs Benedict, sweet sausage, bagels and cream cheese, a waffle lined with strawberries, and a saucer of freshly brewed coffee—with a spread like this, sullying some low-end champagne with OJ might seem ignominious, but it needn't be. With a little thought, the world's Sunday eye-opener can be a paragon of simple beauty.

The Mimosa first glimmered in Parisian hotels in the 1930s, though it was the sixties before the drink found its way onto breakfast tables everywhere. Its recipe was always more suggestion than codified proportion, and early versions were usually a

> 2 ounces fresh-squeezed orange juice
> 4 ounces champagne
>
> → Pour orange juice into a champagne flute, then top up with bubbling joy.

MIMOSA

glass of orange juice with a splash of champagne. Today we know better, and reverse the ratio.

Because the Mimosa has just two ingredients, you have all the more reason to pay special care to them. The champagne needn't be a capital-C bottle (that is, from the French region), but it should be good enough to drink on its own and as dry as possible. For your fruit, Valencia oranges are the unassuming jewels of the market, with more flavorful juice than the pretty navel variety. I've never been known to turn down a blood orange or tangelo Mimosa if you want to try something more exotic, and surely your guests wouldn't either.

BELLINI

When you get down to it, there's hardly a fruit in the world that wouldn't marry well with a tall glass of champagne. But there's something about the cool, mild nectar of a white peach that places the Bellini at the top of the breakfast bar, right next to its citrusy cousin.

The drink dates back almost as far, first created at the recherché Harry's Bar in Venice in 1948. There, Giuseppe Cipriani added a whisper of white peach puree to his champagne flute (well, prosecco flute) and found the pinkish hue reminiscent of the palette of Italian Renaissance painter Giovanni Bellini, and so the name stuck.

Harry's—a gilded haven whose clientele has included everyone from Chaplin to Capote, Hemingway to Hitchcock—has borne not one but two renowned recipes, the other being the plate of thinly sliced raw beef known as carpaccio. And while the Bellini's creative inventors may inspire you to try your own variations on the cocktail, the simplicity of the original is hard to outdo.

canned
peach
puree

1 heaping tablespoon white peach puree*
4 ounces prosecco

→ Add peach puree to a champagne flute,
then top up with prosecco.

* Peach puree surely exists in a fancy grocery somewhere, but making it at
home is as easy as peeling and pitting some very ripe peaches, then whirring in a food processor. The lithe white peach is traditional here, but
fuller-bodied yellow ones are great too. If the peaches aren't as sweet as
you'd like, a touch of honey in the puree is a perfect complement.

FRENCH 75

World War I–era drink, the French 75 is improbably named after the Matériel de 75mm Mle 1897, a quick-firing artillery gun that was sort of an updated version of the cannon from the board game *Risk*. The easy joke is that this booze-on-booze cocktail packs a similar punch, but the French 75 is a

giddy

groggy

pioneering recipe that's worth your attention. It's part sour drink and part champagne drink, essentially a Tom Collins but with champagne in place of club soda. Which makes you wonder what other things can be improved by such a substitution.

1 ounce gin
½ ounce lemon juice
½ ounce simple syrup
3-4 ounces champagne

→ Shake gin, lemon juice, and simple syrup with ice and strain into a cocktail glass. Top with champagne.

GIN AND TONIC

In the early nineteenth century, more than a hundred years before Mary Poppins first prescribed a spoonful of sugar, British colonials in India were doctoring their medicine with hard liquor, splashing gin into their rations. Their tonic, far more bitter than today's varieties, was a homemade mix of club soda, sugar, and quinine extract used to stave off malaria in the South Asian tropics. Today's tonic water contains far less quinine, but that needn't stop one from self-medicating.

2 ounces gin
4 ounces tonic
half a lime

→ Pour gin and tonic into a tall glass over ice, squeeze the lime and drop it in. You may forgo the measurements, naturally.

GIMLET

Meanwhile, while trying to avoid scurvy on the seas, sailors would gin up another medication-turned-mixer: lime juice. The Merchant Shipping Act of 1867 made lime juice a required part of Royal Navy rations, so they turned to a Scotsman named Laughlin Rose to produce a sweetened lime cordial that would preserve the juice at sea.

British sailors, in true fashion, made sure that gin found its way into Rose's lime juice as well. This inspired pairing is attributed to a Navy surgeon named Thomas D. Gimlette, and thus today we have him to thank for the Gimlet. As for the good doctor, he eventually rose to rank of Royal Navy Surgeon General—so it seems his prescription is worth heeding.

2 ounces gin

⅔ ounce Rose's lime juice

→ Shake and strain into a cocktail glass, singing the theme from *H.M.S. Pinafore*.

HOW TO LIKE GIN

I've heard the bullies: "Pine trees." "Wood polish." "Grampa's aftershave." Well, Gin, let me tell you, if they can't appreciate your hinterland bouquet, your fir-lined heights, your peppery verve—then you don't need them either. Only your true friends will ever know the beauty of your marriage with dry vermouth, your truest expression.

But gin in the pantry doesn't have to mean Martinis. London's liquor plays wonderfully with wine-based aperitifs such as Lillet or herbal liqueurs such as Chartreuse. Gin is a friend of the fruit, too—an extra dollop in your next Pimm's Cup is the best way to perk up the lawn cocktail with a fortifying dash of spice.

BEGINNER: GIN PIMM'S CUP (PAGE 126)

Pimm's is already a gin-based liqueur, so augmenting this cocktail with ordinary gin is an easy way to move it in a more juniper direction. Use the regular recipe and add ¾ ounce of gin. A splash of lemonade can help balance out the spice.

ADVANCED: CORPSE REVIVER #2 (PAGE 69)

I've already rhapsodized about why this drink is the essential pick-me-up. It's time for you to try it for yourself.

EXPERT: LAST WORD (PAGE 149)

Briefly forgotten, this 1920s-era cocktail has found its way back into the graces and menus of bartenders today. Both maraschino liqueur and Chartreuse are sweet, but in incredibly weird ways—maraschino with the almond funkiness of cherry pits, and Chartreuse with an apothecary of odd herbs. The result is a drink that's at once alien and very, very refreshing.

MOJITO

Pirates, history teaches us, really did like rum. But for all their swashbuckling machismo, some of these marine-bound marauders could be finicky about their firewater, fancifying it with lime, sugar, and mint.

Early on, the ingredients were muddled with a "medicinal" spirit called aguardiente (literally, "fire water") to create a drink named "Draque" for Sir Francis Drake: sea captain and hero to

SIR FRANCIS DRAKE

the English, outlaw to the Spanish. Over time, the more refined rum replaced aguardiente, and today we have the Mojito.

A word for those who would medicate with Mojitos: Though Drake was just the second man to circumnavigate the globe, he eventually succumbed to dysentery with the best of them, a reminder that mint and lime alone do not count as eating your veggies.

2 ounces light rum
½ a lime, cut into wedges
2 teaspoons sugar
10 or more mint leaves
club soda

➜ In a tall glass, muddle the lime wedges with sugar—this extracts not only the juice but also the aromatic oils locked in the peel. You needn't muddle the mint leaves, just clap them between your hands to bruise them, then add them to the glass. Add ice and rum. Stir, top with club soda, and be prepared to find yourself dancing soon.

SIDECAR

cocktails are one of America's great contributions to culture, iconic as jazz and baseball (the artistic merits of which are a whole other book). But one of the most important cocktails ever invented comes not only from abroad but also from a place that would give a nationalist the shivers: France. The sweet-tart brandy mixture was first shaken up at the Ritz Hotel in Paris in World War I, designed for an odd serviceman who commuted exclusively by sidecar.

Asymmetrical cycle-cars may not be for everyone, but if you commit just one cocktail to memory, make it this one. The Sidecar's proportion of spirit + orange liqueur + citrus juice is the formula for an entire phylum of cocktails, including the Margarita, Kamikaze, and even the maligned Cosmopolitan, which, when unadulterated with fake syrups, is actually tart and delightful.

THE SIDECAR FAMILY

3 parts liquor   2 parts orange liquor   1 part citrus juice

SIDECAR	brandy	cointreau	lemon
MARGARITA	tequila	cointreau	lime
KAMIKAZE	vodka	~~triplesec~~ triple sec	lime

Shake
and
Strain

MARGARITA

The creation legends of the Margarita are too numerous for a book you can hold in one hand. They're also completely unverified, so here's my favorite. This version has a bartender in the 1940s at Tijuana's famous Foreign Club inspired by a dancer named Margarita Carmen Cansino. The concoction was a tart, fiery mix of tequila, orange liqueur, and lime. Ms. Cansino—and this part *is* true—later became known by her stage name, Rita Hayworth, the star of *Gilda*, *Angels Over Broadway*, and the 1941 remake of *Blood and Sand*. It didn't pick up until the 1970s, when tequila gained popularity, but since then it's become a staple at classy parties and tacky restaurants alike.

And you know what else is nice about Margaritas? If you can make a Sidecar, you can make one of these as well. The recipe's the same, only with tequila and lime swapped in for brandy and lemon.

triple
sec

tequila

limeade
concentrate

ice

blend

BLOOD AND SAND

In the 1922 drama *Blood and Sand*, Rudolph Valentino plays a poor young boy who finds fame when he becomes one of Spain's greatest matadors. However, he spoils himself in his newfound success, succumbing to drink and falling into a love triangle that ruins his marriage. His life in shambles, the matador's bullfighting fails as well, and he is gored at the film's end. Fortunately, an unknown 1920s bartender scoffed off the lesson of temperance and honored the film with this ominous-sounding libation. It's an odd coupling of ingredients, to be sure, but all the more fitting for high intrigue.

1 ounce Scotch
1 ounce sweet vermouth
1 ounce Cherry Heering liqueur
1 ounce orange juice

→ Shake like a matador's cape and strain into a cocktail glass.

HOW TO LIKE TEQUILA

Whatever the Margarita has done to elevate tequila's status among the primary liquors, shot glasses and slushy machines have taken away. But tequila's flavors are a vast territory worth exploring. Yes, the vibrant, saline textures of a *blanco* beg for a lime, but they're just as happy alongside grapefruit, dark berries, or even apple cider (*especially* apple cider). Meanwhile, the refined *añejos*, which spend a year or longer aging in oak barrels, are expressive enough to swap in for whiskey in a cozy Old-Fashioned.

BEGINNER: PALOMA (PAGE 133)

The nice thing about this simple cocktail is that you can easily sweeten it to your taste with more grapefruit soda. Or, of course, add more tequila.

collection of shot glasses

ADVANCED: TEQUILA WITH GINGER BEER AND APPLE CIDER

A number of modern bartenders have served their own spin on these flavors, but the basic idea is always the same. Mingled with a spiced cider and the hottest ginger beer you can find, tequila shows off its fiery bite, and at the same time feels downright autumnal. There's no real recipe here; just pour tequila, ginger beer, and cider into a tall glass over ice.

EXPERT: TEQUILA OLD-FASHIONED (PAGE 3)

Old-Fashioneds aren't just for whiskey; you can use sugar and bitters to season just about any spirit. For tequila, you might swap out sugar for agave, which is the base of the tequila-making process. And for a truly educational drinking experience, try a side-by-side comparison of two Old-Fashioneds, one with an unaged *blanco* tequila and one with a *reposado* or *añejo*, and you'll see the wide spectrum of what tequila has to offer.

MARY HUNT

Clearly, as a cocktail writer, I'm in no place to moralize over the effects of alcohol. But in the interest of balance, let's consider Mary Hunt, a leader in the temperance movement in the nineteenth century. An educated woman, Hunt studied at the Patapsco Female Institute in Maryland, where she later was hired as a professor of natural science, researching alcohol's effects on the body. She eventually became the superintendent of the Woman's Christian Temperance Union's education department, leading the effort for drug and alcohol abstinence education in schools. Now, I often abstain from drink—sometimes for several hours at a time—so I thought I'd include a recipe for those dry, trying times.

LAVENDER-HONEY LEMONADE

1 cup honey syrup (dissolve equal parts honey and water)
½ cup simple syrup
½ cup lemon juice
5 cups water
pinch of salt

→ Combine in a pitcher, and garnish with bouquet of fresh lavender and a sense of moral superiority.

salt

lemon

honey

lavendar

simple
syrup

SLOE GIN FIZZ

Growing up, I knew sloe gin as the sticky-capped bottle that collected dust in my parents' liquor drawer. That's what adults drank, I thought. But now England is once again exporting real sloe gin, a funky, tangy liqueur made with sloe berries—which look like blueberry-sized plums and are only marginally edible. But sugar, liquor, and time transform their flavors quite nicely, and this classic long-drink treatment does even more.

2 ounces sloe gin
1 ounce lemon juice
½ ounce simple syrup
club soda

→ Pour ingredients into a tall glass over ice, topping with the club soda. Challenge yourself to drink slowly.

sloe berries

AMERICANO

The Americano owes its creation to the Italian potion-maker Gaspare Campari. And as an American, I am forever indebted to the signore for the honor. Campari is the founder of Gruppo Campari, the progenitor of aperitif spirits such as, well, Campari—and his namesake is this vividly red spirit with the candy sweetness and medicinal bitterness of an orange, from juice to pith.

tanked

The Americano is the essence of the scarlet spirit, mixing glugs of the aperitif and sweet vermouth in a long glass and filling to the brim with sparkling water. The result is a cylinder of stained glass, purely refreshing and radiant. At his bar in Milan, Mr. Campari originally named the drink "Milano-Torino," a nod to the hometowns of his own spirit and his vermouth of choice. But by the turn of the century, when it became popular with the flocks of thirsty, cocktail-savvy American tourists, the Italians welcomed them and renamed the drink in their likeness: Americano.

1½ ounces Campari
1½ ounces sweet vermouth
club soda

➔ Combine ingredients in a tall glass filled with ice. Garnish with an orange slice and be proud of our tourist ancestors.

NEGRONI

The Negroni is yet another cocktail we owe to the good Gaspare Campari, an extension of the Americano. Like so many drinks, it sprung from the demands of a picky customer—in this case, the Florentine Count Camillo Negroni, who one day had the idea of fortifying his Americano with a dose of gin. Naturally, the Negroni name stuck when the drink grew in popularity—such are the benefits of being a count.

I try to be an impartial documentarian, but I have some biases that you should know about. One is that for me, the Negroni is an untouchable cocktail, and I love it more than almost anything else in this book. I hope you don't mind me playing favorites, but here's why I like it so much:

1. It's delicious. Take the sweetness and bitter edge of an Americano, then drape it around the spicy soul of a London dry gin.
2. It's simple. Three ingredients, equal parts. Up or on the rocks? However you please, there's no way to mess it up.

And in its simplicity is a canvas for tinkerers. For example, a classic combination is the quick and cheap Martini & Rossi vermouth and the traditional Beefeater gin accompanying your Campari. They're light selections, and the flavors have room to play together. But in colder months (or harder times), swap in Dolin's silky sweet vermouth and the juniper crunch of Junipero Gin for an aggressive spin on the recipe. And if you *really* want to rankle a cocktail curmudgeon, start switching spirits for whole new ones. Here is the classic recipe, as well as some of my favorite spinoffs.

1 ounce gin
1 ounce sweet vermouth
1 ounce Campari

➔ Combine over ice and garnish with an orange twist. Thank the Count.

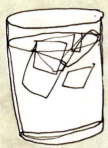

GASPARE CAMPARI
v

BOULEVARDIER

1 ounce bourbon or rye
1 ounce sweet vermouth
1 ounce Campari

→ Combine over ice and garnish with an
orange twist. Thank America. For a
Manhattan-inspired version, double the
amount of whiskey.

OLD PAL

1½ ounces rye
¾ ounce dry vermouth
¾ ounce Campari

→ Stir with ice and strain, and garnish with
a lemon twist. This one's lighter-bodied,
so it's nice served "up."

HANKY PANKY

1½ ounces gin
¾ ounce sweet vermouth
½ ounce Fernet Branca

→ Stir with ice and strain, no garnish. The black-as-night and bitter-as-winter Fernet Branca adds an aggressive bite of menthol to this drink; it's a good introduction to the joys of Fernet, but it's not for the faint of heart.

NEGRONI SBAGILATO

1 ounce sweet vermouth
1 ounce Campari
2 ounces prosecco or sparkling wine

→ Combine over ice and garnish with an orange twist. In Italian, "sbagliato" means "wrong," but replacing gin with a splash of champagne is very, very right.

ANTONIO BENEDETTO CARPANO

After the French, there may be no country more righteous about their wine than the Italians. So imagine the chutzpah of Antonio Benedetto Carpano, who in 1786 thought he would take some of his countrymen's prized white wine and add sugar, liquor, and a witch's pantry of obscure herbs and spices. The outcome, he thought, would be a daintier tipple more suitable for the ladies of the day than the oh-so-manly, uncut white wine.

This was the original form of vermouth, the tawny or red variety that today we call "sweet vermouth." Homemade vermouth was a common staple before Carpano commercialized the process, but nevertheless his family's bottling became the toast of Turin. His wine shop in the Piazza Castello soon became a cafe, and was packed with eager drinkers—of both genders!—waiting for a sip of the wine-based bouquet.

LOUIS NOILLY

Italian vermouth flourished throughout the next century, as the now-famous Cinzano and Martini & Rossi families began production as well. Naturally, the French couldn't stand it.

In 1855, Louis Noilly teamed up with his (English) brother-in-law, Claudius Prat, and began producing his father's recipe for a dry vermouth, with less sugar and herbage. Perhaps this Franco-Anglican heritage is the reason that dry vermouth is today most commonly a condiment for gin and a foil for French sauces, while sweet vermouth is, you know, good for drinking. But let's not take sides.

Bitterness in vermouth comes from the herb wormwood, which also gave the drink its name—in High German, the word for the botanical is "*Wermud*."

RICKEY

From the Sidecar to the Margarita, there's a plethora of cocktails named after bargoers. (The lesson here, it seems, is that pestering your barkeep is the path to eternal fame.) Of these, the Rickey is perhaps the most distinguished.

Col. Joseph Kyle Rickey was a high-profile lobbyist for the Democrats in the 1880s, campaigning for officials including President Grover Cleveland. Now, for those who have never been there, Washington, DC, is a basin of hot air, both politically and meteorologically. So when the Colonel pulled into Shoomaker's, his favorite bar on E Street NW in the shadow of the Capitol, he would order this drink to combat the oppressive heat. Strict historians will note that Rickey himself preferred his long drinks with whiskey, but for anyone who has tried both, the Gin Rickey stands alone as the ideal base for this recipe.

cheers!

Thomas Jefferson Memorial

Washington Monument

The Capitol

1½ ounces gin
half a lime
club soda

→ In a highball glass, pour gin over ice.
Squeeze lime into the glass, drop the
fruit in as well, and top with club soda.
Sip slowly while debating how to handle
the Pullman car workers' strike.

TOM COLLINS

This long drink of gin, lemon, sugar, and club soda is yet another cocktail named after a person. However, the person was a hotel waiter in London named John Collins, and the drink lived under that name for at least a decade before surfacing in Jerry Thomas's 1876 edition under "Tom." This likely happened for two reasons, and one of them is simple enough: The drink was often made with Old Tom gin, the sweetened English variety.

The other reason is that around the same time, an uproarious prank was sweeping the nation, and its name got conflated with the cocktail. The joke may not translate well to our modern-day sensibilities of humor, but I'll see what I can do.

While enjoying the nightlife with companions, probably after a few drinks, you whisper to a friend that you've been hearing some vicious rumors about him. "Rumors?" Yes, rumors, you reply. What's more, the culprit of this vilification is a man named

Tom Collins, and you've heard that he's at another bar down the block right this moment. Your friend, concerned for his reputation and apparently quite gullible, then runs to the next bar, where the bartender, who is in on the prank, tells your friend he just missed Old Tom. And we all have a good laugh.

If that doesn't sound like a grand time to you, you're forgiven. But don't let a bit of flat humor keep you from trying a real Tom Collins—a dash of sugar and a ray of lemon is the perfect way to introduce the unique Old Tom style of gin.

2 ounces Old Tom gin
half a lemon
1 teaspoon simple syrup
club soda

→ In a highball glass, pour gin over ice. Squeeze lemon juice into the glass, discard the fruit, and top with club soda. Before drinking, toast to your friends and swear off unnecessary pranks.

RUMORS?

PIMM'S CUP

When faced with the enviable problem of having too much wine on hand, the resourceful Spanish make sangria, the fruity punch of wine, fruit, sugar, and the occasional sprig of mint. The English, lacking the continent's fertile vineyard land, give the sangria treatment to their own drink of abundance: gin.

In the early nineteenth century, Londoners went frantic for fruit cups, a mixture of liquors, wine, fruit, herbs, and spices. The drink was broadly defined—there were as many combinations as there were bars in London. But one recipe caught a wave of success: the sweet and herbaceous gin liqueur of James Pimm, owner of an oyster bar in the city's center. Soon he began mass producing and bottling his Pimm's No. 1 fruit cup, and by the 1850s the company was devising additional recipes with base liquors of Scotch, brandy, rum, rye, and vodka.

Pimm's Nos. 2-6 have largely been discontinued, but the original Pimm's Cup cocktail is an occasion for creativity. Today this English summer staple is improvised with any number of ingredients, both fizzy (lemonade, ginger ale, or club soda) and fruity (pick a berry, any berry). The most traditional, however, gets a lift of lemon-lime soda and a cooling waft of cucumber.

2 ounces Pimm's No. 1
4 ounces lemon-lime soda
slice of cucumber
sprig of mint

→ In a tall glass, pour Pimm's and soda over ice, then garnish with cucumber and mint. Stir, and when no one's looking, give yourself a splash of regular gin for a pepper kick.

James Pimm

HOW TO DRINK AT WEDDINGS (TWO-INGREDIENT COCKTAILS)

For the ambitious party planner, there is no better exercise in gaiety than a wedding. From the centerpieces—dresses, hors d'oeuvres, and cake—to the manicured ribbons and flowers that peek out at every turn, the meticulous effort that goes into every detail is astounding. Until, of course, you reach the bar.

"Bar" is a generous term for what parched attendees must endure after a five-chorus rendition of "Shout." The embankment itself is a card table or two, cleverly masked by a starchy, white tablecloth so as to resemble a real-life drinking establishment. A well-meaning but frazzled caterer stands guard over their wares: limes, ice, some basic spirits, and a selection of mixers you'd expect from a burglar who had just cracked a vending machine.

These situations call for realistic expectations; don't order a Martini unless you want gin on the rocks. But like a painter limiting his palette, working with constraints can yield simple joys. Stick to two choice ingredients, and you'll discover combinations that will liven the party without flustering the bartender or frustrating the line of guests behind you. These monochrome drinks might not be Blue-era Picasso, but a glass of gin and grapefruit can be refreshing, inspiring, and all you need to keep you buoyant and dancing at your next wedding.

Note: Some of these drinks have proper names as well. However, in unsure circumstances it's best to be straightforward, as you never know when a confused bartender will tragically build a Gin Rickey with Sprite.

BOURBON AND APPLE JUICE

Cider is ideal, but there's a special joy in dressing down your bourbon with a juice-box staple. The result is something like sweet tea and maple syrup, and it's hard not to smile at.

TEQUILA AND APPLE JUICE

Tequila, on the other hand, gets a real makeover when freed of its lime-juice pigeonhole. Its rugged qualities play well with apple juice, coming through like a salty version of rye.

GIN AND GRAPEFRUIT JUICE

Citrus and bite, and everything nice. Grapefruit juice is the holy grail of cheap mixers, the embodiment of the trifecta of sweet, sour, and bitter. Mix it with pink or mix it with yellow, this is the only wedding drink you'll ever need.

TEQUILA AND GRAPEFRUIT JUICE

When you get down to it, grapefruit juice is good in just about anything. Mix it with tequila, and you approach the tartness of a

Margarita. Add a splash of Sprite, and you essentially have a Paloma.

RUM AND GRAPEFRUIT JUICE

See page 129. Even grapefruit juice can't fully mask the funky sunscreen flavor of cheap rum, but at a wedding, this is as close as you'll get to a Papa Doble.

RUM AND COLA

Of course.

GIN AND SELTZER, EXTRA LIMES

By now, most wedding bartenders know that "soda" means "bubbly water" and not a sweet drink, but I still say "seltzer" to be safe (plus, it's fun to say). It's breaking the rule to add a third ingredient, but think of it as doing the bartender a favor—someone had to cut all those limes, and they're probably glad to put them to use.

SWEET VERMOUTH AND DRY VERMOUTH

This one might fetch you some strange looks, but if you can bring yourself to order it, you'll be rewarded with an herbaceous, medium-sweet aperitif that's a staple at many a French or Italian sidewalk cafe.

Paloma

Every year on May 5, Americans celebrate Mexican heritage by shrugging off their New Year's resolutions and giving tequila another shot. Unfortunately, this often includes actual shot glasses. But for the binge-averse and Margarita-weary, there's another option for tequila that marries the sprightly agave spirit with citric tang.

La Paloma (Spanish for "the Paloma"*) is as simple as cocktails get, a soda-age combination like the rum-and-Coke. But by pairing tequila with grapefruit's eye-widening complexity, the recipe is a public service announcement for the unfairly maligned liquor. The low-maintenance soda version is a fine place to start, but switch to fresh-squeezed grapefruit juice, and you'll never use another shot glass again.

juice
of half
a lime

---

* actually translates to "pigeon" or "dove"

PALOMA

2 ounces tequila
half a lime
grapefruit soda

➔ Combine ingredients in a tall glass with ice. (For tequila shoppers: *añejo* is the longest-aged, *reposado* is medium-mellow, and unaged *blanco* is feistier.) The grapefruit soda should be a Mexican variety like Jarritos; save your Fresca for visiting relatives.

La Paloma, the paloma translates as the pigeon

FRESH PALOMA

2 ounces tequila
juice of half a grapefruit
juice of half a lime
splash of agave nectar or simple syrup
pinch of salt (why not?)
club soda

→ Combine over ice in a tall glass. This
  version is marginally fancier, but stay
  calm. Don't sweat the measurements,
  and let the spirits guide you.

spill

LONG ISLAND
ICED TEA

Sorry if this comes as a shock to you, but I'm going to tell you how Long Island Iced Teas are made. It might be cruel, like taking a child to a hot dog factory, but hopefully by now you've grown up, you're reading books about cocktails, and your tastes are ever so slightly more sophisticated than draining every bottle in the pantry into your biggest cup and topping it with Coke. You won't be able to unlearn this, so if Santa Claus and the Tooth Fairy were enough of a revelation for you, cover your eyes and turn to the next page.

Because we're all adults, this version includes fresh lemon juice, though strict traditionalists should buy a bottle of sour mix and keep it in the back of the fridge for three months before using.

1 ounce vodka
1 ounce gin
1 ounce rum
1 ounce tequila
1 ounce triple sec
1¼ ounces fresh lemon juice
½ ounce simple syrup
cola

PRETEND...

FAT
FLOUR
BEEF
MEAT
ONION
SPICE
CORN
EGG
CHICKEN
SALT
PORK

→ Shake everything but the cola with ice, strain into a pint glass filled with ice, and top with cola. Drink with a curly straw while doing something you'll regret. Repeat as necessary.

DON THE BEACHCOMBER

I f you've ever sipped a cocktail out of a fake coconut, or a fake bamboo stem, or a fake totem pole, you have Don the Beachcomber to blame—although if Don himself had made you the drink, you'd probably be thanking him.

Don the Beachcomber (born with the mellifluous name Ernest Raymond Beaumont-Gantt) pioneered the American tiki bar, opening his place by the same name in Hollywood in 1934. Back then, it had all the trappings you'd recognize today: hula music, chintzy Polynesian decor, and fruit-and-rum cocktails laden with parasols and ambrosial garnish. The trend thrived for three decades, fueled by enthusiasm from Hollywood and nostalgia for the South Pacific brought by American soldiers returning home. Copy-

cats flourished as well, including the well-known Trader Vic's chain that helped spread the rum craze nationwide.

Don left Hollywood to serve in the Army in World War II, during which time his wife, "Sunny" Sund, expanded the Beachcomber into a chain. When they divorced after the war, she kept the chain, while he moved to Hawaii and opened another Don the Beachcomber, complete with the familiar straw and bamboo—and, reportedly, a resident myna bird trained to squawk, "Give me a beer, stupid!" Then, in 1959, Hawaii was granted U.S. statehood. I assume they raised tiki mugs in celebration.

ZOMBIE

At a glance, the Zombie might look like a kitchen-sink cocktail, a Long Island Iced Tea with a Bahama bent. But it carries two important distinctions: 1) the recipe, which is a secret to this day, was slavishly perfected by Don the Beachcomber, and 2) at Don's bar, at least, you were only allowed one.

Don the Beachcomber recorded his recipes in notebooks filled with hand-scrawled code, which cocktail historians like the modern-day author Jeff Berry have tracked down and untan-

1½ ounces light rum
1½ ounces dark rum
½ ounce overproof rum
1 ounce lime juice
1 ounce pineapple juice
1 ounce guava nectar (or another tropical juice)
½ ounce grenadine
2 dashes Angostura bitters

→ Shake with ice and strain into a tall glass over crushed ice. Begin lounging.

gled with some success. Many ingredients were referred to only by number, others by names like "Don's Mix," which Berry has determined to be two parts grapefruit juice and one part cinnamon syrup.

So it seems that Don the Beachcomber's true, original Zombie recipe is a lost treasure, perhaps squirreled into a hollowed-out Bible somewhere, or rolled up and hidden in an antique picture frame. Whatever the case, historians and bartenders have fallen for and tinkered with this recipe enough times that we have some excellent secondhand versions to enjoy.

DAIQUIRI

When trying new drinks, a good rule of thumb is that whenever you come across an adapted recipe with a name like "strawberry _____," you should try the original first. And so it is with the Daiquiri. Since its supposed invention in Cuba (though really, rum and lime is as obvious a pairing as peanut butter and jelly), the drink has been fed countless new fruits and flavorings, and today is most often seen behind the window of a slush machine, where it is sentenced to eter-

2 ounces light rum
1 ounce lime juice
½ ounce simple syrup

→ Shake with ice and strain into a cocktail glass. Upon the last sip, turn around and make a Papa Doble.

nal whirring. But before the blender age, the Daiquiri was a study in simplicity: just rum, treated as it was meant to be. If you've never experienced the quietude of a light rum at home in its element, this is the place to start.

PAPA DOBLE

Now that you've passed Daiquiri 101, it's time to move up to the master's level—and the undisputed master of the Daiquiri is Ernest Hemingway. Camped in Cuba, specifically on a stool at a Havana bar called El Floridita, he worked on his consumptive reputation, for both quantity and for taste. Being in Cuba he was naturally going to be drinking Daiquiris, but being Hemingway, he was not going to wile away days sipping anything so ordinary.

His signature drink, named from his nickname ("Papa") and the deftness with which he consumed them (in doubles), is a marvelously vibrant cocktail that begins as a Daiquiri and improves

upon each ingredient, one by one. Lime juice finds a new friend with the more complex grapefruit. Ordinary sugar takes the form of rich maraschino liqueur. And if you're Hemingway, a shot of rum becomes two shots. (Though for safety's sake, here is a more sociable version.)

2 ounces light rum
1 ounce lime juice
½ ounce grapefruit juice
⅓ ounce maraschino liqueur

→ Shake with ice and strain into a cocktail glass, or into a tall glass over crushed ice. Blending this drink is allowed, and even encouraged; if you do, a bit more lime and maraschino liqueur will keep the flavors buoyant through the ice.

Make mine a double.

ERNEST HEMINGWAY
a.k.a
PAPA

AVIATION

There's no better celebration of maraschino's marzipan twang than the Aviation, where the liqueur plays Bonnie to gin's Clyde, the two of them racing under a lemon sun. Its three ingredients are so outspoken, so apart from one another, it's a wonder that they combine at all. And indeed, they seem to take turns within each sip: The gin leads with brawn, then re-

---

2 ounces gin
½ ounce maraschino liqueur
½ ounce lemon juice
dash of crème de violette (optional)

➜ Shake with ice and strain into a cocktail glass.
If you've already purchased a jar of maraschino
cherries, stow them away until your next bar
mitzvah, where they'll make a fine
accompaniment to a Shirley Temple.

---

cedes as the sweet maraschino floats through, only to be clipped by the lemon's tartness. This is a drink with a character arc.

Strict historians will hunt down a bottle of the obscure (but increasingly available) crème de violette, which adds a note of petals and turns the cloudy drink a marvelous dawn-purple. But even without, this cocktail is the perfect introduction to the world of maraschino—and, dare I say, gin as well.

BONNIE & CLYDE

LAST WORD

The Last Word is a drink at odds with itself. It's composed of four incongruous ingredients, in equal parts, and each seemingly pulling in a different direction. In one corner is spicy gin, and adjacent to that, an acidic squeeze of lime. Across the spectrum you have two syrupy sweet liqueurs: amandine maraschino and the high-octane herbal digestif Chartreuse. On paper the combination might sound mad, like a child's concoction from a soda fountain, but in perfect balance, this cocktail emerges rich, heady, and rewarding.

¾ **ounce gin**
¾ **ounce lime juice**
¾ **ounce maraschino liqueur**
¾ **ounce green Chartreuse**

➔ Shake with ice and strain into a cocktail glass. Behold the drink's dense, green hue, and dive in.

RUSTY NAIL

The Rusty Nail is a gift to the home bartender: two ingredients, hard to forget, and impossible to ruin. The "recipe"—or notion, you might say—appeared under many names in the first half of the twentieth century before the Rusty Nail stuck in 1963. But you needn't remember anything besides this: Scotch and Drambuie.

In Scotch, you have the bottled peat of the Isles; in Drambuie, a bottled kit for Scotch Old-Fashioneds. The liqueur is a mixture of Scotch, honey, and motley herbs and spices—the transatlantic

---

2 ounces Scotch (typically a blended variety)
1 ounce Drambuie

→ Stir in a short glass over ice, lemon twist
optional. Halfway through, top up with
splashes of both.

cousin of the whiskey-sugar-bitters trinity. From smoky Islays to the malty Highlands, whiskies are as varied as drinkers' personal tastes, so use this recipe as a mere starting point (adjusting, of course, with extra pours).

HOW TO LIKE WHISKY (U.K. VERSION)

Somewhere between Winston Churchill and Gordon Gekko, Scotch became Dad's drink, the liquor of choice for high-flying businessmen and their in-flight catalogs. It's easy to see how at first sniff, they might all seem identical: rough, aggressive, smoky. But once you get used to a baseline cinder, you unlock the world of malted barley, the same milky sweetness you find in a malt ball or milkshake. Then again, for some of us, the smoke itself is the perfect payoff.

BEGINNER: BLOOD AND SAND (PAGE 101)

With three sweet ingredients to tamp down the smoke, this film-inspired cocktail is friendlier than it sounds. It's almost a dessert drink, but it will have you mixing up a second batch.

ADVANCED: RUSTY NAIL (PAGE 150)

Again, this drink is nowhere near as harsh as it sounds—something about the smoky dram just begets angry-sounding cocktail names. Here, the spirit is perked with Drambuie, a Scotch-based liqueur that's spiced and sweetened with honey.

EXPERT: WHISKEY SKIN (PAGE 159)

Connoisseurs might balk at the thought, but if you're not dealing with a fancy bottle, heating up a Whiskey Skin is a lovely way to unlock the spirit's malty sweetness. Spiced toddies and the like are fun too, but it's amazing how much complexity you can find with simply Scotch, sugar, and water.

POUSSE CAFÉ

How do you mix up a Pousse Café? You don't—Pousse Cafés are layered drinks, made by painstakingly floating liquids of different densities into separate, visually striking, and virtually unenjoyable strata, making them the perfect drink for someone with nothing better to do. Here's an example from the 1860s or so that came from the New Orleans cafe Santina's Saloon:

1 part cognac
1 part maraschino liqueur
1 part curaçao

➔ In a tall, fussy glass, start with a bit of cognac, then carefully layer the maraschino by pouring it over the back of a spoon. Finish by using your new spoon technique to float the curaçao on top. If executed perfectly, you should have a glass of syrupy, sweet, warm liqueurs. Delicious, right? Stand back and take some photos of your magnificently stratified cocktail, because it does indeed look beautiful, and you'll never want to make one again.

The Coen brothers drink white russians

WHITE RUSSIAN

Whatever historical events surround the creation of the White Russian of the 1960s, they are obscured by March 6, 1998, the day directors Joel and Ethan Coen unleashed a disheveled, disarranged, and druggedly disembodied Jeff Bridges upon the world in their film *The Big Lebowski*. Bridges's character, known cosmically as "The Dude," is snapped from his routine of day-drinking and night-bowling when he is thrust into a plot of kidnapping and mystery—at the expense of a treasured rug—as a result of mistaken identity. The road is not without its tolls, but waiting at the end is liquid sustenance of vodka, Kahlua, and cream; and so, The Dude abides.

2 ounces vodka
1 ounce Kahlua
splash of cream

→ Combine over ice and abide.

HOT TODDY

As early as the 1700s, long before the first cocktails, civilized drinkers were unlocking the deep aromas and soul-warming glow of the Hot Toddy. The ingredients were, and still are, as simple as could be: spirit, sugar, and hot water, in amounts to taste. The liquor was most commonly whiskey, although whether Scotch, Irish, American, or rye was a matter of debate. But the colonials weren't choosy with their hooch, and brandy, rum, applejack, and the occasional Dutch gin (a mellow, sweet variety) were all reasonable stand-ins.

In his book, the legendary Jerry Thomas skirts the fracas by providing essentially identical recipes for versions with each spirit. Then, he goes on to describe several "Slings," which are the same as Toddies but with a grating of fresh nutmeg. And then, he describes yet another hot drink called a "Skin," which is the same thing again but with a lemon peel, and seemingly only fit for Scotch whiskey.

Not to downplay the impact of a twist of lemon, but this is about as useful as recipes for coffee, coffee with milk, and coffee with milk and sugar.

It's certainly more complication than we need to keep track of today, when our hot-drink mixing can be informed by more than a century of cocktail culture. The sugar can become any number of spice or fruit syrups, not to mention honey, agave, and molasses. Hot water can become black tea, green tea, a sweet chamomile, or a smoky Lapsang Souchong. The combinations are too many to list, so relax and play with what's in your cupboard. Just don't forget, from time to time, to return to the classics.

2 ounces brandy
6 ounces hot water
1 teaspoon sugar

➔ Fetch slippers and stoke the fireplace.
   Combine in a mug and stir.

WHISKEY SKIN

2 ounces Scotch
6 ounces hot water
1 teaspoon sugar
lemon peel

→ Combine Scotch, water, and
sugar in a mug, twist peel into
mug, and stir. Enjoy.

ACKNOWLEDGMENTS

For me, this is very much a Washington, DC, book, and I owe thanks to many people in that hotbed of good writing. To my editors at *Washington City Paper*, Andrew Beaujon, Tim Carman, and Chris Shott, my real mentors. To Erik Wemple, who thought it'd be a good idea to hire a beer writer, and to everyone who's ever haunted that crazy place. Thanks to the bartenders who humored me, especially Dan Searing, who always had time for a story and some cheap brandy. On the New York team, thank you to my agents, Stephanie and Anna; my editor, Marisa; and my adviser, Beth.

Thank you to my family and friends, who listen supportively when I prattle, even when I'm not making them drinks, and often after a small amount of coffee. Thank you to the patrons of Saint Bernard, the coziest bar that never existed on Perry Place.

And, of course, thank you to the amazing Elizabeth Graeber. Your turn, Elizabeth:

I had so much fun working on the illustrations for this book, and am extremely proud with how it turned out. A huge thank-you to Orr, Gernert, and Gotham Books. And to my family, friends, and everyone who encourages me to keep drawing, thank you!

ABOUT THE AUTHORS

Former speakeasy operator **ORR SHTUHL** is a writer and drinker (not always in that order) who for three years penned the Beerspotter column for the *Washington City Paper*. His work has also been featured on NPR and in major daily newspapers. He lives in Brooklyn.

ELIZABETH GRAEBER is an illustrator who graduated from the Maryland Institute College of Art in 2007 and is currently living in Washington, DC. Projects include illustrations for the USPS website, the Phillips Collection and *The Washington Post.* In 2012 she was named DC's best local illustrator by the *Washinton City Paper.* Everywhere she goes she carries a sketchbook to draw what she sees. You can find her work at www.elizabethgraeber.com. Her favorite cocktail is a mint julep.

INDEX

Note: Page numbers in italics refer to illustrations.

absinthe
    Brooklyn, 18–19, *20*
    Corpse Reviver #2, 69, 93
    fountains, *63, 64,* 66
    spoons, *64*
agave nectar, 105, 134
aguardiente, 93
American Revolution, 52
Americano, *110,* 111–12
añejo tequila, 103, 105, 133
Angostura bitters
    Manhattan, 7–8
    Martini, 25
    Old-Fashioned, 3–4
    Zombie, 140–41
apple cider, 103, 129
apple juice, 129
applejack, 46, 55, 157–58
Astor mansion, 44
Aviation, 23, *30,* 147–48

bar equipment, 58–67, *59, 61*
Beaumont-Gantt, Ernest Raymond, 139–40
Becker, Charles, 44
Beefeater gin, 113
beer, 50

Bellini, 81–83
Bellini, Giovanni, 81–82
berries
    Daiquiri, 143–44
    Mimosa, 78–79
    Pimm's Cup, 126–27
    and sloe gin, 108, *109*
    and tequila, 103
Berry, Jeff, 140–41
The Big Lebowski (1998), 155
bitters
    Bronx, 13–15
    Manhattan, 7–8
    Martini, 25
    Old-Fashioned, 3–4, 105
    Zombie, 140–41
blanco tequila, 103, 105, 133
blended Scotch, 150–51
Blood and Sand (cocktail), 101–2, 151
Blood and Sand (film), 2, 98, *100,* 101
blood oranges, 79
Bloody Mary, 72–75
Blue Blazer, 41–42, *43*
Bond, James, 30
bootlegging, 70
Boston shakers, 59, *59, 61*

Boulevardier, 116
bourbon, 21
    and apple juice, 129
    Cherry Bounce, 50–51
    Mint Julep, 32–33
    Old-Fashioned, 3–4
brandy
    Cherry Bounce, 50–51
    Corpse Reviver #1, 69, 93
    Fish House Punch, 54–56
    Hot Toddy, 157–58
    Jack Rose, 21–23
    Pimm's Cup, 126–27
    Sidecar, 97
Bridges, Jeff, 155
Bronx cocktails, 13–15, 17–18
Brooklyn, 18–19, 20
buying bar equipment, 58–67

Campari
    Americano, 110, 111–12
    Boulevardier, 116
    Negroni, 113
    Negroni Sbagliato, 117
    Old Pal, 116
Campari, Gaspare, 111, 112, 115
Cansino, Margarita Carmen, 2, 98
Carpano, Antonio Benedetto, 118
Casino Royale (2006), 30
champagne, 78–79, 85–86. See also
  prosecco
Chartreuse Gin, 91, 93, 149
Cherry Bounce, 50–51, 51
Cherry Heering liqueur, 101–2
Churchill, Jeanette, 7
cider, 18–19, 55, 105
Cipriani, Giuseppe, 81
citrus juicers, 60, 61
citrus juices, 37, 96–97. See also specific
  citrus fruits
Cleveland, Grover, 121

club soda
    Americano, 110, 111–12
    French 75, 85–86
    Fresh Paloma, 134
    Gin and Tonic, 86–87
    Gin Rickey, 121–23
    Mojito, 93–94
    Paloma, 103, 131–33, 134
    Pimm's Cup, 126–27
    Rickey, 121–23
    Sloe Gin Fizz, 108, 109
    Tom Collins, 86, 124–25
Coca-Cola, 132, 136
cocktail picks, 63, 65
Coen brothers, 154, 155
cognac, 152–53
Cointreau
    Corpse Reviver #2, 69, 93
    Margarita, 96–97, 98–99
    Sidecar, 97
cola, 131, 132, 136–37
Collins, John, 124
Corpse Reviver #2, 69, 93
Cosmopolitan, 96
coupes, 60, 62
Craddock, Harry, 69
Craig, Daniel, 30
cream drinks, 155
crème de violette, 147–48
Cuba, 143–44, 145
cucumber, 126–27
curaçao, 152–53

Daiquiri, 143–44
dark berries, 103
Don the Beachcomber, 139–40
Drake, Francis, 93–94
Drambuie, 150–51
"Draque," 93–94
dropper bottles, 64, 66
Dry Martini, 23–25, 26–27, 30

dry vermouth
    Bronx, 13–15
    Brooklyn, 18–19, *20*
    Old Pal, 116
    origin of, 119
    and wedding bars, 131
Duplex, 15
Dutch gin, 157–58

El Floridita, 145
elements of cocktails, 1
equipment for bartending, 58–67, *67*

Fenet Branca, 117
Fish House Punch, 54–56
flaming drinks, 41–42, *43*
Flanagan, Betty, 52
Foreign Club, 98
French 75, 85–86
Fresh Paloma, 134
fruit cups, 126. *See also* Pimm's Cup
fruit juices. *See also specific fruits*
    Bellini, 81–83
    and gin, 91
    Mimosas, 78–79

gender discrimination, 52
Gimlet, 89–90
Gimlette, Thomas D., 89
gin
    Aviation, 23, 147–48
    Bloody Mary, 72–75
    Bronx, 13–15
    Corpse Reviver #2, 69, 93
    Dutch gin, 157–58
    French 75, 85–86
    Gimlet, 89–90
    Gin and Tonic, 86–87
    and grapefruit, 129
    Hanky Panky, 117
    Last Word, 93, 149
    London Dry gin, 25, 30, 112–13

Long Island Iced Tea, 136–37
    Martini, 23–25, 66
    Negroni, 112–13
    Pimm's Cup, 91, 126–27
    and seltzer water, 131
    Sloe Gin Fizz, 108, *109*
    Tom Collins, 86, 124–25
Gin Rickey, 121–23
ginger ale
    Brooklyn, 18–19, *20*
    Pimm's Cup, 126–27
ginger beer, 105
grapefruit
    and gin, 129
    Paloma, 103, 131–33, 134
    Papa Doble, 131, 143, 145–46
    and rum, 131
    and tequila, 103, 129–31
grenadine
    Jack Rose, 21–23, 46
    Zombie, 140–41
Gruppo Campari, 111
guava nectar, 141

hangover cures, 69
Hanky Panky, 117
Harry's Bar, 81–82
Hawaii, 140
Hawthorne strainers, 59, *59, 61*
Hayworth, Rita, 2, 98
Hegeman, Maurice, 18
Hemingway, Ernest, 145
Highland Scotch whiskies, 151
honey, 83, 106, 150, 152, 158
hot drinks, 157–59
hot sauce, 72–75
Hot Toddy, 157–58
Hotel Nassau, 18–19
How to Mix Drinks, or the Bon Vivant's
    Companion (Thomas), 38–39, *40*
Hunt, Mary, 105–6

ice crushing bags, 63
ice picks, 63
infusions, 50–51
Inverse Manhattan, 23
Islay Scotch whiskies, 151

Jack Rose (cocktail), 21, 44–46
Jacquemot rose, 44
Jarritos soda, 133
jiggers, 59, *59, 61*
juicers, 60, *61*
julep strainers, 63, *65*
Junipero Gin, 113

Kahlua, 155
Kamikazes, 96–97

Last Word, 93, 149
Lavender-Honey Lemonade, 106, *107*
layered drinks, 152–53
lemon-lime soda, 127, 131
lemons
    Aviation, 23, 147–48
    Blue Blazer, 41–42
    Bronx, 13
    as cocktail staple, 13, 73
    Corpse Reviver #2, 69, 93
    Fish House Punch, 54–56
    Hot Toddy, 157–58
    Jack Rose, 21–23, 44–46
    Lavender-Honey Lemonade,
      106, *107*
    Long Island Iced Tea, 136–37
    Martini, 25
    Old Fashioned, 3–4
    Old Pal, 116
    Pimm's Cup, 91, 126–27
    Rusty Nail, 150–51
    Sidecar, 97
    Sloe Gin Fizz, 108, *109*
    squeezing fresh, 37

    Tom Collins, 86, 124–25
    Whiskey Skin, 158, 159
Lillet Blanc, 31, 69
limes
    as cocktail staple, 13
    Daiquiri, 143–44
    Gimlet, 89–90
    gin and seltzer water, 131
    Gin and Tonic, 86–87
    Gin Rickey, 121–23
    Kamikaze, 97
    Last Word, 149
    Margarita, 96–97, 98–99, 103
    Mojito, 93–94
    Paloma, 103, 131–33, 134
    Rose's lime juice, 89–90
    squeezing fresh, 37
    Zombie, 140–41
liquor, 1–2
London Dry gin, 25, 30, 112–13
long glasses, 63, *63, 65*
Long Island Iced Tea, 136–37

Manhattan, 7–8, 23, 27, *30,* 58–59
maraschino liqueur
    Aviation, 147–48
    Dry Martini, 27
    Last Word, 93, 149
    Papa Doble, 131, 143, 145–46
    Pousse Café, 152–53
Margarita, 96–97, 98–99, 103
Martinez, 25, 26–27
Martini
    bar equipment for, 58–59
    equipment for mixing, 66
    glass for, *30*
    history of, 23–25
    stirring vs. shaking, 30
Mary Hunt, 105–6
mason jars, *64,* 66
McCoy, Bill, 70, *71*

measuring liquors, 66
Merchant Shipping Act, 89
Metropolitan Hotel, 38
Milano-Torinos, 111
Mimosas, 78–79
mint
    Mint Julep, 32–33
    Mojito, 93–94
    Pimm's Cup, 126–27
Mojito, 93–94
Mount Vernon, 48
muddlers, 60, *61*

Negroni, 112–13
Negroni, Camillo, 112
Negroni Sbagilato, 117
New York Times, 18
Noilly, Louis, 119

Old Pal, 116
Old Tom gin, 24–25, 124–25
Old-Fashioned
    bar equipment for, 58–59
    history of, 3–4
    mixing instructions, 3, 23
    and syrups, 27
    with tequila, 105
orange bitters, 15, 25, 26
orange liqueur, 96–97, 98
oranges
    Blood and Sand, 101–2
    Bronx, 13–15
    Campari, 111
    Manhattan, 7–8
    Mimosas, 78–79
    Screwdrivers, 77
    squeezing fresh, 37
origins of "cocktail" term, 3

Paloma, 103, 131–33, 134
Papa Doble, 131, 143, 145–46

Patapsco Female Institute, 106
peach brandy, 56
peach puree, 81–83
Petiot, Fernand, 72
pewter mugs, *62,* 63, *65*
Pimm, James, 126, *127*
Pimm's Cup, 91, 126–27, *127*
pineapple juice, 141
pirates, 93
Planter's House, 38
Pousse Café, 152–53
Prat, Claudius, 119
Prohibition, 70
prosecco, 83, 117
punch recipes, 50, 54–56
punch sets, 63

quinine, 87

reposado tequila, 105, 133
Revolutionary War, 52
Rickey, 121–23
Rickey, Joseph Kyle, 121, *123*
Ritz Hotel, 96
Rose, Jack, 1–2, 44, *45. See also* Jack
    Rose (cocktail)
Rose, Laughlin, 89
Rosenthal, Herman, 44
Rose's lime juice, 89–90
Royal Navy, 89
rum
    and cola, 131
    Daiquiri, 143–44
    Fish House Punch, 54–56
    and grapefruit juice, 131
    Hot Toddy, 157–58
    Long Island Iced Tea, 136–37
    Mojito, 93–94
    overproof rum, 141
    Papa Doble, 131, 143, 145–46
    and tiki bars, 139–40

Zombie, 140–41
Rusty Nail, 150–51
rye whiskey
    Boulevardier, 116
    George Washington and, 48–50
    Hot Toddy, 157–58
    Manhattan, 7–8
    Old Pal, 116
    Old-Fashioned, 3–4

sangria, 126
Santina's Saloon, 152–53
Schmidt Cafe, 18
Schuylkill Fishing Company, 54–56
Scotch whiskey
    Blood and Sand, 101–2
    Blue Blazer, 41–42, 43
    Rusty Nail, 150–51
    Whiskey Skin, 158, 159
Screwdrivers, 77
seltzer water, 65, 66, 131
sexism, 52
shakers, 59, 59
Shoomaker's, 121
shot glasses, 104
simple syrup
    Blue Blazer, 41–42
    Daiquiri, 143–44
    Fish House Punch, 54–56
    French 75, 85–86
    Fresh Paloma, 134
    Lavender-Honey Lemonade, 106
    Long Island Iced Tea, 136–37
    making, 35–37
    Mint Julep, 32–33
    Old-Fashioned, 3–4
    Sloe Gin Fizz, 108, 109
    squeeze bottles for, 60, 61
    Tom Collins, 124–25
"Skins," 158, 159
"Slings," 157–58

Sloe Gin Fizz, 108, 109
smuggling, 70
social clubs, 54–56
Solon, Johnnie, 15
sparkling wine, 117. See also
    champagne; prosecco
speed pourers, 63
spiced cider, 105
spices, 72–75
Sprite, 129, 131
squeeze bottles, 60, 61
State in Schuylkill (angling club), 54–56
stirring vs. shaking, 30
strainers, 59, 59
sugar. See also simple syrup
    Cherry Bounce, 50–51
    Hot Toddy, 157–58
    Mint Julep, 32–33
    Mojito, 93–94
    and original Martinis, 24–25
    simple syrup, 35–37
    Tom Collins, 86, 124–25
    Whiskey Skin, 158, 159
Sund, "Sunny," 140
sweet vermouth
    Americano, 110, 111–12
    Boulevardier, 116
    Bronx, 13–15
    Brooklyn, 18–19, 20
    Hanky Panky, 117
    Manhattan, 7–8
    Martinez, 25, 26–27
    Martini, 24–25
    Negroni, 113
    Negroni Sbagilato, 117
    origin of, 118
    and wedding bars, 131
swizzle sticks, 62, 63

Taft, William Howard, 15, 16, 17–18
tangelos, 79

tea, 54–56
tea strainers, 60, 62
temperance movement, 106
tequila
    and apple juice, 129
    with ginger beer and
        apple cider, 105
    and grapefruit juice, 129–30
    Long Island Iced Tea, 136–37
    Margaritas, 96–97, 98–99, 103
    Old-Fashioned, 105
    Paloma, 103, 131–33, 134
Thomas, Jerry, 38–39, 41, 124,
    157–58
three-part shakers, 63
Tijuana, 98
tiki bars, 139–40
Tilden, Samuel J., 7
Tom Collins, 86, 124–25
tomato juice, 72–75
tonic water, 1, 86–87
Trader Vic's, 140
Trapier, William Heyward, 32
triple sec, 97, 136–37
tumblers, 60, 61

University of Oxford, 32
U.S. Supreme Court, 52

Valencia oranges, 37, 79
Valentino, Rudolph, 101–2
vermouth
    Americano, 110, 111–12
    Blood and Sand, 101–2
    Bronx cocktails, 13–15
    Brooklyn, 18–19, 20
    history of, 119
    Inverse Manhattan, 23
    Manhattan, 7–8
    Martinez, 25, 26–27
    Martini, 24–25, 27, 66

Negroni, 113
    origin of, 118
Vespers, 30
vodka
    Bloody Mary, 72–75
    Kamikazes, 97
    Long Island Iced Tea, 136–37
    Pimm's Cup, 126–27
    Screwdrivers, 77
    Vesper, 31
    White Russian, 155

Waldorf Astoria, 15, 19
Washington, DC, 121, 122, 161
Washington, George, 48, 49, 50, 55
Washington, Martha, 50, 50
weddings, 128–31
whiskey. See also rye whiskey;
    Scotch whiskey
    Blood and Sand, 101–2, 151
    Hot Toddy, 157–58
    Inverse Manhattan, 23
    Jack Rose, 21–23, 44–46
    Manhattan, 7–8
    Mint Julep, 32–33
    Old-Fashioned, 23
    Rusty Nail, 150–51, 152
    Whiskey Skin, 152
    Whiskey Skin, 158, 159
    White Russian, 155
    wine, 118. See also vermouth
    wine refrigerators, 64, 66
    Woman's Christian Temperance
        Union, 106
    women bartenders, 52
    Worcestershire sauce, 72
    wormwood, 119, 119, 120

zesters, 60, 61
Zombie, 140–41